Talk Like a
Californian

TALK LIKE A CALIFORNIAN

A HELLA FRESH GUIDE TO GOLDEN STATE SPEAK

Sweet.

Prospect Park Books

HELENA VENTURA

CONTENTS

Introduction 5

Say It Right 6

A Word About Freeways 8

STATEWIDE 9

NORTHERN CALIFORNIA 25

SOUTHERN CALIFORNIA 55

HOLLYWOOD SPEAK 91

SURF SLANG 121

TECH TALK 137

Index of Terms 164

THE REAL CALIFORNIANS

Despite what you see on SNL, there's more to talking like a legit Californian than freeway names and "dude"—although don't get us wrong, those are essential. But California-speak is so much richer. If you're going to live in LA, for instance, you're going to hear Hollywood slang, even if you never set foot on a studio lot. If you'll be spending any time in Silicon Valley, Silicon Beach, or the Mission, you'll want a basic knowledge of tech talk. And surf speak is so pervasive that it's influenced how people talk nationwide.

Then, of course, there's the popular slang that has its roots in either Northern or Southern California, from hella and grippa to fresh and no bueno. And then there are all the places and things to know about! What's the difference between the Delta breeze and June gloom? Who plays at the Stick or the Roaracle? Where are OB, PV, DP, and SC? And, perhaps most importantly, how do you pronounce Jamacha, Sepulveda, and San Rafael?

All this knowledge is found within this little book. Please explore and enjoy. Yee!

SAY IT RIGHT

The Golden State is rich with Spanish names, and most are pronounced the way they'd be in Spanish: El Cajon (CA-hone), Santa Ynez (EE-nez), Mojave (moe-HAH-vay), San Clemente (kleh-MEN-tay). Exceptions abound, however, and there are plenty of other unusual pronunciations. If you want to sound like a legit local, study this list.

BERNAL (HEIGHTS): BURR-nul

CABRILLO: Cah-BRILLO in San Francisco, but Cah-BREE-oh everywhere else

CLEMENT (STREET): Kluh-MENT

CONCORD: KON-kerd

CUYAMACA: Kwee-ah-mahk-uh

DUBOCE: Duh-BOWS

ESTUDILLO (AVENUE): Ess-stew-DILL-oh

GOUGH (STREET): Goff

GUERNEVILLE: GERN-vill, although some say GERN-ee-vill

JAMACHA: HAM-ah-shaw

JUNIPERO: You-NIP-err-oh

KEARNY: Kern-ee

LA JOLLA: Lah HOY-ah

LOS FELIZ: Lahs FEE-liss

LOS GATOS: Lahs GAA-toes

MARIN: Mah-RIN

LOMPOC: LOHM-poke

NICASIO: Nih-KASH-oh

NOE: NOH-ee

OTAY: Oh-tai

PHELAN: FEEL-ihn

PLACENTIA: Plah-CENT-cha

POINT REYES: Point Rayz

PORT HUENEME: Port why-NEE-mee

POWAY: POW-way

RODEO (DRIVE & BEACH): Roh-DAY-oh

SAN LUIS OBISPO: San LEW-iss Oh-bis-poh

SAN RAFAEL: San RAH-fell

SEPULVEDA: Se-PUL-veh-duh

SUISUN CITY: Soo-SOON (leave out the "City")

VALENCIA: Vah-LEN-cha

A WORD ABOUT FREEWAYS

First of all, if it has on-ramps and off-ramps, it's a freeway, not a highway. Pacific Coast Highway (PCH) has no ramps, so it's a highway; the 101 is a freeway in many sections, but in some parts of the state it becomes a highway. New to parts of California are toll roads, which are freeways that are not free. They're called simply "toll roads."

Secondly, it's essential to know that in Southern California, all freeways are preceded by the word "the": the 101, the 5, the 605, the toll road. And yet you should never ever call PCH "the PCH."

This changes in Central and Northern California. People will say "Highway 99" in the San Joaquin Valley, and somewhere north of Goleta, the 101 becomes simply 101. In the Bay Area, you do not put a "the" before a freeway number—you'd say, "Go south on 101, and then take 156 to Highway 1."

ANIMAL STYLE

Perhaps the most popular term from In 'n Out's secret menu: an animal-style burger has mustard-grilled patties and extra dressing and pickles. Animal-style fries have Thousand Island dressing, cheese, and grilled onions.

I'll take a 3x3 animal style.

THE BIG ONE

The massive quake that's going to hit the Bay Area or Southern California any minute now.

My husband wants us to move to Portland before the Big One hits.

We're picking up my sister in Phoenix and taking the RV to Cali for the Rose Parade.

CALI

A word for California that no Californian will ever use; it's as horrible as saying "Frisco" to a San Franciscan.

DANK

Traditionally, to inhale marijuana smoke, but more frequently used as an adjective to describe something exceptionally good.

> Have you had the paleo brownies at Urth? They're dank.

DUDE or DUE

A substitute for a person's name, and the father of all modern Southern California slang. "Dude" is rooted in surf culture but is now used universally. Originally used just between guys, it is now gender-neutral. If used with a period, it means, "I agree."

Dude, that new ramen place in Truckee is epic.

That selfie is fire.

FIRE

Hot (as in hip); often expressed with a fire emoji.

Can you bring guac and chips to the Oscars party?

GUAC

Guacamole,
the state dish
of California.

I'm driving Uber and dogsitting as my side hustles.

HUSTLE

Your work.

JUNE GLOOM & MAY GRAY

The damp marine layer that blankets Southern California in late spring and early summer; in San Francisco, June gloom is heavy fog.

The June gloom is bumming me out— let's go to the desert.

Oooh, you're hella moded.

MODED

To have been proven wrong in an embarrassing way, or caught doing something, or shut down.

I'm jonesing for a big ol' pocho burrito from El Tepeyac.

POCHO, POCHA

People of Mexican descent who don't speak Spanish and are considered to have lost their culture; also used for food and cultural references.

PRIDE

The gay pride parade in San Francisco; to a lesser extent, the one in West Hollywood.

SKETCH

When something appears to be questionable, illegitimate, or deliberately misleading.

SUS

Short for "suspicious," has replaced "sketch" with most people under 40.

Katie says the sushi at Ralphs is great, but I think it looks sus.

YEE

Yeah. The Bay Area claims it as its own, but it's statewide now.

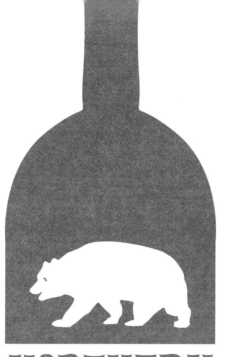

NORTHERN
CALIFORNIA

A FEW REGIONAL NICKNAMES

THE 415 — San Francisco

ACROSS THE BAY — the East Bay,
to San Franciscans

THE AVENUES — the Richmond and the Sunset
districts west of Twin Peaks in San Francisco

THE BAY — the San Francisco Bay Area

BORAGA — Moraga

CAL — UC Berkeley

CITY — San Francisco City College

THE CITY — San Francisco

CV — Castro Valley

DOCO — Downtown Commons in Sacramento

DP — Dolores Park in San Francisco

THE DUB-C — Walnut Creek

EASTSIDE O — East Oakland

FILLMOE, THE MOE — Fillmore

FIVE & DIME — East Bay (510 area code)

THE HAIGHT — Haight-Asbury

HIPPIE HILL — the meadow at the beginning of Golden Gate Park

M-TOWN — Milpitas

THE CASTRO, THE MISSION, THE PRESIDIO, THE RICHMOND, THE SUNSET — various San Francisco districts

MOUNT TAM — Mount Tamalpais

OAKTOWN OR THE TOWN — Oakland

THE ROCK — Alcatraz Island

SACTOWN — Sacramento

SILICON VALLEY, THE VALLEY — the Santa Clara Valley south of San Francisco

SOUTH CITY — South San Francisco

SQUALLYWOOD — Squaw Valley in Tahoe

STATE — San Francisco State University

UC — UCSF Hospital (not the university)

WINE COUNTRY — Napa and Sonoma counties

THE YAY — the Bay Area

BEEZY

A woman: a betty, a broad, a bitch, a ho. Sometimes derogatory, sometimes not.

Me and my beezies are gonna rage at Outside Lands next weekend.

The Comical has never been the same since Herb Caen died.

The COMICAL

The San Francisco Chronicle.

You can't even get a Lyft out in that cutty hood.

CUTTY

Sketchy, dicey, possibly unsafe, or a place out in the sticks.

DELTA BREEZE

An evening breeze coming off the Sacramento and San Joaquin rivers that brings some relief in Sacramento and the Central Valley's killer summer heat.

> I'd never survive Sactown if it wasn't for the Delta breeze.

DUBS

The Golden State Warriors.

The Dubs better take care of Steph if they know what's what.

DUSTY

Ugly and/or badly dressed.

EMERALD TRIANGLE

The cannabis-growing capital of the U.S., comprising Humboldt, Trinity, and Mendocino counties.

Caleb says he's working at a startup in the Emerald Triangle, but it sounds sus to me.

I'm finna get fish tacos at Comal— you in?

FINNA

About to, or going to.

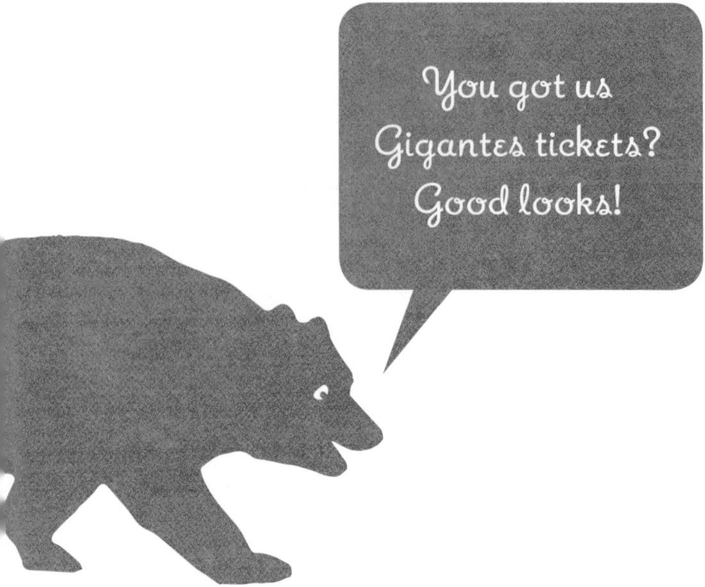

GOOD LOOKS

Thank you.

GRIP, GRIPPA

A good quantity of something.

Get me a grippa fries when you're at Park.

HELLA

The mother of all modern Northern California slang, hella means "really" or "very." **South Park** says it's out of date, but you'll hear it nonetheless.

Cancun's burrito is hella awesome.

HYPHY

Hyper, rowdy; originally a style of high-energy hip-hop music and dance in Northern California. Some say it's only used ironically now.

I'm juiced for Bay to Breakers—this year I actually trained.

JUICED

Pumped up, excited, stoked.

KARL the FOG

The name of San Francisco's notorious fog. Karl has hundreds of thousands of Instagram and Twitter followers.

LOS GIGANTES

The San Francisco Giants.

Los Gigantes got a hella good shot this year.

> She's so deep in the Marin bubble that she just gave her therapist a Tesla for Christmas.

MARIN BUBBLE

The wealthy, entitled, PC culture in Marin County.

Elle quit her job at the PR place to open a dog boutique on Fillmore with daddy's money. What a Marina girl.

MARINA GIRL

The ultra-attractive, moneyed, hard-partying, Instagram-loving, yoga-pants-wearing, often-ditzy girl who lives in San Francisco's Marina District.

MISSION-ISTAS

Hip young folks, typically in tech, who have been gentrifying the Mission in San Francisco.

Rents are so insane that the Missionistas are living four to a one-bedroom.

PAINTED LADIES

The colorful row of Victorian houses on Alamo Square.

How original— my mom's watercolor class is setting up at the Painted Ladies.

ROARACLE

Oracle Arena.

SHARKIES

The San Jose Sharks hockey team, whose home rink is nicknamed the Shark Tank.

SLAPS

An upbeat, party-friendly song.
"Slapper" is the matching adjective.

Matt's got the slaps for the party in Oaktown tonight.

THE STICK

Candlestick Park.

We got rained out
at the Stick.

SWOOP

To pick someone up.

The Mission is crawling with tech douchebags drinking Anchor Steam boilermakers.

TECH DOUCHEBAG

A tech worker in the Bay Area.

TRYNA

Trying to.

> I'm tryna get a rezzie at Commis.

YADDADI-MEAN

You know what I mean?

I'm over that beezy, yaddadimean?

A FEW REGIONAL NICKNAMES

THE 626 OR THE SGV — the San Gabriel Valley

THE BAS — Calabasas

THE BOARDWALK — the paved path along Venice Beach

THE BOWL — the Hollywood Bowl

BURBANK AIRPORT — Bob Hope Airport (no one calls it that)

THE CANYONS — The three canyon streets (Coldwater, Laurel Canyon, Beverly Glen) that connect the Valley to LA

DIRTY DENA — Altadena

EAST LOS — East LA

THE INLAND EMPIRE — Much of Riverside and San Bernardino counties east of LA

JOHN WAYNE — John Wayne Airport in Santa Ana

K-TOWN — LA's Koreatown

LBC — Long Beach

THE MARINA — Marina del Rey

NASTY CITY — National City

NOHO — North Hollywood

NORTH COUNTY — North San Diego County

OB — Ocean Beach

THE PALISADES — Pacific Palisades

PB — Pacific Beach

THE POINT — Point Loma

PQ — Rancho Peñasquitos

PV — Palos Verdes

SC — USC

THE SHAW — Crenshaw

SILICON BEACH — Santa Monica to Playa del Rey

THE SOUTH BAY — Manhattan Beach to Palos Verdes Estates

SOUTH PAS — South Pasadena

TJ — Tijuana

THE VALLEY — San Fernando Valley in LA and Mission Valley in San Diego

909er

Someone who lives in the Inland Empire, where the area code is 909; often used to signify low-class hicks.

Get those 909er kooks outta here.

Ohmygod, the blue crab roll at Sugarfish is literally the best ever.

Bible.

BIBLE

Kardashian-speak for "that's the truth."
Syn.: word.

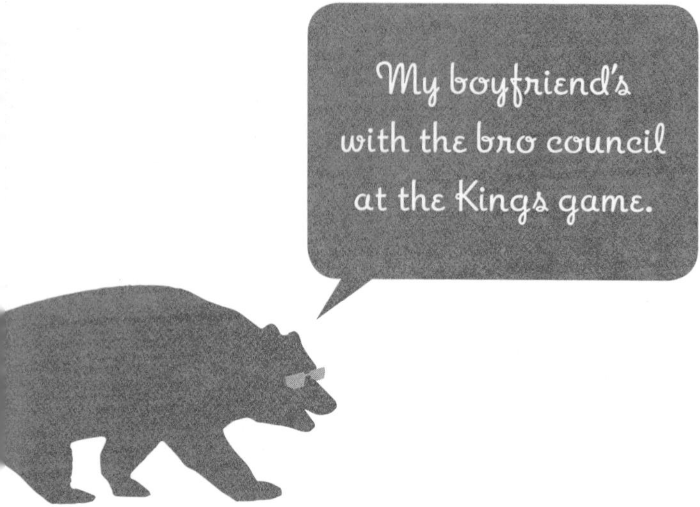

BRO COUNCIL

Boys' night out.

CEDARS

Cedars-Sinai hospital, almost always referred to as Cedars.

The DEL

The iconic Del Coronado Hotel
on San Diego's Coronado Island.

My great-grandparents
were married at the Del,
and my family has gone
there for Labor Day
every year since.

My girlfriend's taking me to the Ace in the desert for my birthday.

The DESERT

Palm Springs and environs. No one ever says, "I'm going to the desert" and means Mojave.

I got a ticket for flippin' a bitch in the middle of La Cienega.

FLIP A BITCH

To make a sudden u-turn.

The FOUR LEVEL

LA's most famous freeway interchange, where the 101 and the 110 tangle up on the north edge of Downtown.

> There's a sigalert at the Four Level.

FRESH

Cool, stylish, current.

Your haircut is fresh.

Can't hear the Doyers game over those damn ghetto birds.

GHETTO BIRD

A police or news helicopter.

GHETTO BLUE

The Metro Blue Line, which connects downtown LA and Long Beach.

Take the Ghetto Blue and I'll meet you in LBC.

GHETTO DOG

Bacon-wrapped hot dogs sold from street carts, especially in the Fashion District area of downtown LA.

Let's get some pastor from la troca.

LA TROCA

Spanglish for "the truck," as in the beloved taco truck.

LEGIT

Excellent, awesome.

LOS DOYERS

The Dodgers.

I've been stuck at the Merge for an hour.

The MERGE

The always-congested intersection of the 5 and the 805 in San Diego.

Vin Scully's mo is eternal.

MO

Short for moment;
when someone is living
his or her best life.

NO BUENO

"No good" in San Diego and many beach towns.

The Chargers were no bueno tonight.

OMW

On my way.

Because you're always stuck in traffic.

Maddie wants to dye her hair purple, but that's so not on brand for her.

ON BRAND

Something that fits your style/brand.

The Orange Crush is a nightmare—Angels and Ariana Grande on the same night.

The ORANGE CRUSH

Where the 5, the 57, and the 22 meet in Anaheim.

PCH

Pacific Coast Highway;
never say "the PCH."

PROGRAM

Describing a person in a 12-step program.

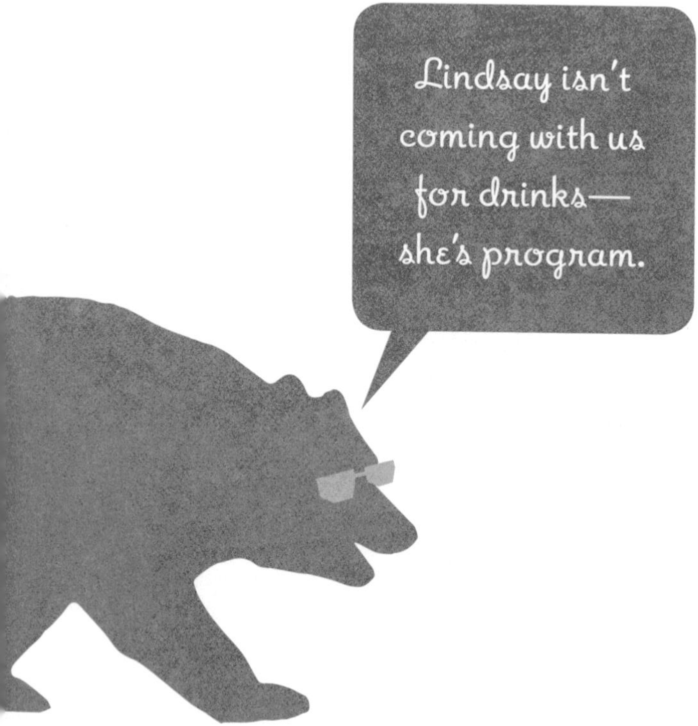

SAMO, SAMOHI

Santa Monica High School, pronounced SAA-moe or SAA-moe-hai

SANTA ANAS

The fire-starting winds from hell that hit Southern California in the fall.

"It was one of those hot dry Santa Anas that come down through the mountain passes and curl your hair and make your nerves jump and your skin itch. On nights like that every booze party ends in a fight."

— Raymond Chandler

There's a Sigalert for the 405 between the 10 and the 105.

SIGALERT

A CHP notification of a traffic problem.

Can't ride in my convertible Mini without my stunnas.

STUNNAS

Sunglasses, typically large and showy ones.

SUP EY?

"What's up?" in Spanglish.

SWEET

A term of approval:
really nice, quality, and/or beautiful.

The Local Natives show was tightsauce.

TIGHTSAUCE

Outstanding and/or attractive.

Look at Amanda's gels—
she's such a Val.

VAL

A resident of the San Fernando Valley.
More popular in the 1970s and '80s
(see: Moon Unit Zappa's song "Valley
Girl"), but still meaningful.

YAS

You go girl! Add
as many extra
'a's as you like.

I'm not wearing
a bra tonight.

Yaaas
queen!

ZONIES

Arizonans and other desert dwellers who come to San Diego in the summer.

Let's go to the movies—too many Zonies at the beach.

10-100

When someone on
set has gone to pee,
sometimes shortened
to 10-1. Guess what
10-200 is?

Hold for five—
Leo's 10-100.

It's an above the line party, with a few token crew for atmosphere.

ABOVE THE LINE

Hollywood's power people: directors, writers, producers, and actors. It's a term from early movie days, when the salaries for those key people were put "above the line" on the budget. Below the line folks are the working stiffs: camera, makeup, editing, lighting, etc.

AD, PA, AP, UPM, EP

> The EP told the AD that she's pissed that the PA forgot the lime La Croix.

Job titles are uniformly shortened in Hollywood: AD for assistant director, PA for production assistant (or personal assistant), AP for associate producer, UPM for unit production manager, EP for executive producer, etc.

Get those damn bogies out of there!

BOGIES

People who might walk into a shot— or who do walk into a shot.

Read these 12 scripts and get me coverage by the morning.

COVERAGE

A studio reader's or agent's assistant's summary of a script. Also means the different angles a director shoots.

CRAFTY

The craft-service person—sometimes the full caterer but sometimes just the snacks-and-drinks provider. Crafties provides the kale chips, seaweed, Oreos, almonds, and, most importantly, every flavor of La Croix ever invented.

> *What's your 20? Crafty has Häagen-Dazs bars!*

DESK

Assistant to
an agent or
production
company.

Entry-level job.
Must have at
least one year's
desk experience.
(A recurring
oxymoron in
Hollywood job
listings.)

> You have a 3:15 with Staci. There'll be a drive-on at Gate 3.

DRIVE-ON

A parking pass that allows you to drive on the studio lot, instead of parking in that huge structure two blocks away and walking onto the lot like a barney.

FLYING IN

When something or someone is coming back to set quickly.

> Can someone get a kombucha with a straw for Zoey?

> Copy, flying in.

FOLEY

Sound effects added
in post-production.

We'll have to add
the footsteps in
foley.

GOLDEN TIME

Super-duper overtime, which typically kicks in for union workers after 16 hours.

The show is killing me, but the good news is I'm naming my new boat The Golden Time.

Emily's green, but she's super-smart, so she'll pick it up.

GREEN

A novice in the industry.

Where's Jenny?

She's either in video village or in the green room.

GREEN ROOM

The room in which the talent waits before going onto a talk show, or the room on a sitcom stage in which the suits are stashed to keep them off of the stage; filled with sushi as an incentive.

HAVING HAD

Having finished your meal.

Call time's 7 a.m. having had.

HIATUS

Unemployment.

I'm just helping out at my friend's restaurant while I'm on hiatus.

Wardrobe has an espresso machine in their honeywagon— they'll make you a shot.

HONEY-WAGON

Trailers that house production, wardrobe, dressing rooms, etc. Portapotties are often on the back of them.

LOCK UP

When the PA or AD secures the set before the camera rolls.

We're ready to go— lock up.

MARTINI SHOT

The final set-up for the last shot of the day; an Abby Singer (named for a famed AD) is the second-to-the-last shot.

I'm going out with the 2nd AD for tequila shots after the martini shot.

NOTES

Comments made on a script, a performance, a cut, or almost any part of the creative process.

Post-production:
editing, sound
editing, mixing.

SCRIPTY

A script supervisor, who's the note-taking liaison between the director and the editor.

> Watch out, scripty's in a mood today.

SHOPPING

Pitching a script or series around town.

I'm just making a few bucks at Intelligentsia while my writing partner and I shop our script.

The show is lame, but the showrunner is a mensch, so I'm in it for the long haul.

SHOW RUNNER

The head honcho on a TV show, almost always either the show's creator or the head writer.

STEPPING ON

When an actor or other VIP walks onto the stage, or when people talk over each other on walkie-talkies or in a performance.

Heads up—Galifianakis is stepping on.

Tell the AD to get the suits off the set and back in the green room where they belong.

SUITS

Network and studio executives, who try to assert their authority over T-shirt-clad writers and directors by wearing Paul Stuart suits.

I've buffed and shined my treatment— time for my agent to shop it.

TREATMENT

A narrative, prose summary of a script; in commercials, the pitch a director sends to the ad agency.

VIDEO VILLAGE

The collection of monitors that the director, writer(s), and producer(s) huddle around to see what the cameras are shooting.

> It's looking tense over in video village.

WHAT'S YOUR 20?

Where are you? Almost always spoken into a walkie-talkie, aka a walkie.

Cocktails after the martini shot— what's your 20?

SURF SLANG

AGGRO

Annoyingly aggressive.

BARNEY

An uncool beginner who gets in the way, a kook.

Eh brah, you got time for a Stella?

BRAH

Hawaiian pidgin for "bro" or "dude." A skater variant is "bruh."

EGGY, EGG

Dull, blah, boring.

Let's bounce, these waves are egg.

EPIC

Exceptional, grander, or more impressive than normal.

The Patio makes an epic barley-kale-manchego-pickled fig bowl.

> Outside Lands just released the lineup— it's gonna be firing this year.

FIRING

When the surf is great. Can be used to refer to anything else that's performing in top form. Syn: cranking, epic, going off.

GANDOLF

An older, wiser guy.

GOING OFF

Great waves,
outstanding
surfing, or
doing anything
at your peak.

The dolphins were going off on the trip to Catalina.

INSANE

Beyond good.

Mammoth's pow-pow is gonna be insane.

KOOKS

Amateurs, kids, the inexperienced.

Best Coast was rad at the Greek last night.

RAD, RADICAL

Impressive, awesome.

SHRED

To surf a wave exceptionally well.

> I bet you totally shredded that job interview.

SICK

Fantastic.

Dude, are you going to that party in Dirty Dena? I'm so stoked.

STOKED

Excited, fired up.

WORKED

To get thrashed in the surf,
or in a wipeout in any sport.

10X

Pronounced "ten-ex," this refers to either a whiz-kid programmer who can do the work of ten others, or the minimum annual growth rate that a VC wants to see in a startup.

Joey's app is genius, but no way does it have 10x potential.

Word is they're funding an apportunity for doggie day care.

APP-ORTUNITY

An app in development that promises to make an everyday task easier.

BAND-WIDTH

Either temporarily overloaded, brain-wise, or permanently a few cards short of a deck.

That brogrammer barely has enough bandwidth to code a Pong game.

Don't even think about doing a startup until you take Reid Hoffman's blitzscaling class at Stanford.

BLITZ-SCALING

Growing a software company as fast as possible, by any means possible, to capture market share.

Let's bounce—
this party is just a bunch
of brogrammers from
Snapchat.

BRO-GRAMMER

A programmer who's more of a frat boy than a nerd. This increasingly common male is known to throw around "bro" and pitch for his tech company's softball team.

CHURN RATE

The percentage of customers who quit using your app or service, or the percentage of new hires who quit.

> With a churn rate like that, they'll be lucky to survive until June.

DEMO DAY

When startups in an
accelerator program
pitch their product to
investors.

I'd rather parachute
into North Korea than
face another demo day
like that one.

Can't come to Tahoe this weekend— I have to stay home and dogfood the new app.

DOGFOODING

Testing/using your own product before releasing it to the public; short for "eating your own dog food."

They're cray-cray if they think they can gamify that chemo-organizing app.

GAMIFICA-TION

Adding game-like components to an otherwise non-fun program or app.

HACK

To figure out a shortcut solution to a problem. It also means to illegally gain access to information stored in digital devices and/or databases.

She's got an awesome hack for making mole negro in 30 minutes.

LIFESTYLE COMPANY

A business that is merely successful and profitable.

> It sounded like a great job, but I turned it down— it's just a lifestyle company.

> That ninja is taking the semester off from the 8th grade to code for us.

NINJA

A superstar talent in tech, usually younger than 25.

OFF THE GRID

Disconnecting from devices, the internet, and possibly your job.

Maggie's going off the grid at the end of Q4 to drive her boyfriend's van from Seattle to Ecuador.

Ping me when you get to the hackathon.

PING

To get in touch with someone or get their attention.

PIVOT

Your startup didn't fail—
you're just pivoting in a
new direction.

PRE-REVENUE

A startup with no actual income.

It's pre-revenue, but I'm super-stoked at the potential.

RAMEN PROFITABLE

A startup that is profitable only because the founders live in an uncle's basement and eat ramen.

Sure, they're profitable, but only ramen profitable.

We will absolutely hit a 10x return if we can just get another six months of runway.

RUNWAY

How much money your startup has left before you crash into the failure wall. Usually measured in terms of months, as in how many months of overhead (rent, salaries) you have left.

SLACK

Named for the hot chat tool, it has come to be a verb meaning to send something: a piece of code, a funny GIF, or an emoji.

> The guy in sales I kissed at the bar last night just slacked me a winky face. Awkward.

Tyler's cocktail app is super sticky.

STICKY

When an app or product has a high user retention.

My CEO came back from her thought-leadership cruise babbling on about cross-functional process and radical practicality.

THOUGHT LEADER

A visionary with the big ideas.
Syn.: poseur, phony.

THREE COMMAS CLUB

Members have a net worth in three commas range—as in a billion.

He's still living with his parents even though he just joined the three commas club.

THE UBER OF

Shorthand for something that has potential to disrupt an industry to a fabulously successful degree.

She's funding a startup that's supposed to be the Uber of plumbing.

I can't even go to that Philz anymore— too many unicorns hogging the tables.

UNICORN/ DECACORN

Before 2013, start-up companies with an estimated value of over $1 billion were as rare as finding a unicorn. Now, unicorn/decacorn companies/people can be found grazing by the dozens in Silicon Valley.

Adam's kind of a barney, but his dad's a VC, so I'm going out with him again.

VC

A venture capitalist: can make all your dreams come true or crush them.

WANTRE-PRENEUR

A wannabe tech entrepreneur who doesn't actually have any good ideas.

Mommy's money is burning a hole in that wantrepreneur's pocket.

INDEX OF TERMS

10-100, 92
10x, 138
415, the, 26
626, the, 56
909er, 58
above the line, 93
Across the Bay, 26
AD, PA, AP, UPM, EP, 94
aggro, 122
animal style, 10
apportunity, 139
Avenues, the, 26
bandwidth, 140
barney, 123
Bas, the, 56
Bay, the, 26
beezy, 28
Bernal Heights, 6
bible, 59
Big One, The, 11
blitzscaling, 141
Boardwalk, the, 56
bogies, 95
Boraga, 26

Bowl, the, 56
brah, 124
bro council, 60
brogrammer, 142
Burbank Airport, 56
Cabrillo, 6
Cal, 26
Cali, 12
Canyons, the, 56
Castro, the, 27
Cedars, 61
churn rate, 143
City, 26
City, the, 26
Clement Street, 6
Comical, the, 29
Concord, 6
coverage, 96
crafty, 97
cutty, 30
Cuyamaca, 6
CV, 26
dank, 13
Del, the, 62

Delta breeze, 31
demo day, 144
Desert, the, 63
desk, 98
Dirty Dena, 56
DoCo, 26
dogfooding, 145
DP, 26
drive-on, 99
Dub-C, the, 26
Duboce, 6
Dubs, 32
dude or due, 14
dusty, 33
East Los, 56
Eastside O, 27
eggy, egg, 125
Emerald Triangle, 34
epic, 126
Estudillo Avenue, 6
Fillmoe, the Moe, 27
finna, 35
fire, 15
firing, 127
Five & Dime, 27
flip a bitch, 64
flying in, 100
foley, 101
Four Level, the, 65
fresh, 66
gamification, 146
gandolf, 128
ghetto bird, 67
Ghetto Blue, 68

ghetto dog, 69
going off, 129
golden time, 102
good looks, 36
Gough Street, 6
green, 103
green room, 104
grip, grippa, 37
guac, 16
Guerneville, 6
hack, 147
Haight, the, 27
having had, 105
hella, 38
hiatus, 106
Hippie Hill, 27
honeywagon, 107
hustle, 17
hyphy, 39
industry, the, 108
Inland Empire, the, 56
insane, 130
Jamacha, 7
John Wayne, 56
juiced, 40
June gloom & May gray, 18
Junipero, 7
K-town, 57
Karl the fog, 41
Kearny, 7
kooks, 131
La Jolla, 7
la troca, 70
LBC, 57

legit, 71
lifestyle company, 148
lock up, 109
Lompoc, 7
Los Doyers, 72
Los Feliz, 7
Los Gatos, 7
Los Gigantes, 42
M-town, 27
Marin, 7
Marin bubble, 43
Marina girl, 44
Marina, the, 57
martini shot, 110
Merge, the, 73
Mission, the, 27
Missionistas, 45
mo, 74
moded, 19
Mount Tam, 27
Nasty City, 57
Nicasio, 7
ninja, 149
no bueno, 75
Noe, 7
NoHo, 57
North County, 57
notes, 111
Oaktown, 27
OB, 57
off the grid, 150
OMW, 76
on brand, 77
Orange Crush, the, 78

Otay, 7
Painted Ladies, 46
Palisades, the, 57
PB, 57
PCH, 79
Phelan, 7
ping, 151
pivot, 152
Placentia, 7
pocho, pocha, 20
Point Reyes, 7
Point, the, 57
Port Hueneme, 7
post, 112
Poway, 7
PQ, 57
pre-revenue, 153
Presidio, the, 27
Pride, 21
program, 80
PV, 57
rad, radical, 132
ramen profitable, 154
Richmond, the, 27
Roaracle, 47
Rock, the, 27
Rodeo (Drive & Beach), 7
runway, 155
Sactown, 27
Samo, Samohi, 81
San Luis Obispo, 7
San Rafael, 7
Santa Anas, 82
SC, 57

scripty, 113
Sepulveda, 7
SGV, the, 56
Sharkies, 48
Shaw, the, 57
shopping, 114
showrunner, 115
shred, 133
sick, 134
Sigalert, 83
Silicon Beach, 57
Silicon Valley, 27
sketch, 22
slack, 156
slaps, 49
South Bay, the, 57
South City, 27
South Pas, 57
Squallywood, 27
State, 27
stepping on, 116
Stick, The, 50
sticky, 157
stoked, 135
stunnas, 84
Suisun City, 7
suits, 117
Sunset, the, 27
sup ey?, 85
sus, 23
sweet, 86
swoop, 51
tech douchebag, 52
thought leader, 158

three commas club, 159
tightsauce, 87
TJ, 57
Town, the, 27
treatment, 118
tryna, 53
Uber of, the, 160
UC, 27
unicorn/decacorn, 161
Val, 88
Valencia, 7
Valley, the, 27, 57
VC, 162
video village, 119
wantrepreneur, 163
what's your 20? , 120
Wine Country, 27
worked, 136
yaddadimean, 54
yas, 89
Yay, the, 27
yee, 24
Zonies, 90

SHOUT OUTS

Helena Ventura is an amalgam of many awesome Californians, all of whom were essential to creating this book. They are: Colleen Dunn Bates, Darryl Bates, Emily Bates, Dorie Bailey, Ava Burton, Katie Buderwitz, Lindsay Cook, Lisa Eltinge, Dawn Fanning Moore, Christian Workman, and Ellie Workman. Snaps also to Caitlin Ek and Elizabeth Ovieda.

Copyright © 2017 by Prospect Park Books

Published by
PROSPECT PARK BOOKS
2359 Lincoln Ave.
Altadena, CA 91001
www.prospectparkbooks.com

Library of Congress Cataloging in Publication Data
is on file with the Library of Congress

Printed in the United States of America

Design by
Kathy Kikkent